Life
Mastery

A GUIDE FOR CREATING THE LIFE YOU
WANT AND THE COURAGE TO LIVE IT

JOEL D. ANASTASI

With Channel Jeff Fasano

ISBN: 0983143331
ISBN-13: 9780983143338

Adapted/Written by Joel D. Anastasi and Channeled by Jeff Fasano

angelnewsnetwork@gmail.com

DEDICATION

To those who wish to make the most of their lives
and are willing to do what it takes to make their
dreams come true. You know who you are.

YOU ARE AN IMMORTAL SOUL
HERE FOR A SHORT TIME.

ENJOY IT.

DARE.

PULL OUT OF YOUR FEAR AND DOUBT,
AND LIVE YOUR LIFE.

HAVE THIS EXPERIENCE.

— QUADO

YOUR TIME HERE IS LIMITED.

DON'T WASTE IT LIVING SOMEONE ELSE'S LIFE.

DON'T BE TRAPPED BY DOGMA,
WHICH IS LIVING ACCORDING TO OTHER PEOPLE'S THINKING.

DON'T LET THE OPINIONS OF OTHERS
DROWN OUT YOUR OWN INNER VOICE.

MOST IMPORTANT, HAVE THE COURAGE
TO FOLLOW YOUR HEART AND INTUITION.

SOMEHOW THEY KNOW WHAT YOU TRULY WANT TO BECOME.

— Steve Jobs, Founder Of Apple Corp.

Contents

Introduction

Most of us believe we are here for a *purpose*. And if you're anything like me, you may have spent a good deal of your life trying to figure out what that purpose is.

I have been a student or a presenter of life/career planning programs a good deal of my life. I have seen people from widely different backgrounds, ranging from poor minorities to wealthy senior corporate executives, struggle with the same core questions:

- Who am I?
- Why am I here?
- What should I be doing with my life?

We ask these questions because we want to be happy and fulfilled in our personal lives and careers. We want to figure out what our life paths should be and muster the *courage* to follow them.

It may appear simplistic to think that a mere life/career planning program can help achieve those challenging goals, but if any program can, I believe this one can. The management and human-development programs I have worked with professionally usually have been created by people associated with the field of *psychology*. This program was not.

Life Mastery is *divinely inspired*. It comes from the Archangelic Realm of Michael.

I developed the *Life Mastery* program from channeled messages from Archangel Michael received through trance channel Jeff Fasano. Trance channels are able to go into a trance, allowing another energy or spirit to enter their body and use their voice to speak.

Jeff had his first channeling experience on his forty-fourth birthday in 2002 when he channeled the Archangel Michael. Since then he has channeled many spiritual entities from the highest dimensions of the divine realms. Jeff, to me, is one of the most powerful spiritual channels of our time and a true gift to mankind's spiritual growth and evolution.

Spiritual channeling was not new to me when I encountered these materials. I had spent most of the first decade of this century becoming quite familiar with channeling while writing my book *The Second Coming, The Archangel Gabriel Proclaims a New Age*. *The Second Coming* records my conversations with the Archangel Gabriel channeled by trance channel Robert Baker. I am a trained journalist. I found channel Robert Baker completely credible and my experience with Archangel Gabriel powerful.

Jeff and I met through Robert Baker and were now part of a group of five men, a precursor to the Angel News Network (see links page), who were preparing for a spiritual journey to Mt. Shasta in 2010. The trip was guided by channeled instructions from the Archangel Michael, who asked us to prepare for our journey by reviewing teachings Michael had presented through Jeff a few years earlier.

As I reviewed the material, I soon realized that it covered subjects included in many outstanding management development programs I had worked with in corporate America. However, the lectures and exercises took the students far deeper into their psyches than any programs I had encountered.

Initially, I adapted this material into a twelve-lesson self-study program. Concurrently, Jeff was channeling additional teachings from Michael, which he later published as *Journey of the Awakened Heart: Discovering Your Passion and Purpose*. I have taken material from that book and expanded *Life Mastery* into its current sixteen-lesson format. (I recommend Jeff's book if you wish to learn more about the channeling experience and for its rich, clear content.)

The result, in my view, is the finest program dealing with life/career issues I have seen. Indeed, it is far more than that. To me, not only has Michael given us a brilliant *guide for living*, but I believe this program also can justly be described as a great manifesto of *human freedom*.

Why? My answer relates to the spiritual *context* Michael offers for these teachings. (This program works whether you resonate with the spiritual context or not.)

Michael teaches that each of us comes to this earthly plane as an individual soul with a *mission* to learn life lessons we ourselves have chosen. This mission is part of our "divine soul plan." (The soul is the individuated personification of God that lives within each human being.) Beginning in early childhood, our consciousness usually becomes so shaped and distorted by the influence and conditioning of others (family, culture, authority figures, etc.) that most of us lose sight of who we are and why we are here.

"You have displaced your power and greatness," Michael says. "You have given yourself away and put yourself in the hands of others. It is time to go *inside* to find your *authentic self,* so that you may *discover* and *be* who you are. Through this process you will be *deactivating* the old conditioning of the nervous system and *retraining* it into the beingness of the self."

That, essentially, is the mission of the Life Mastery program: *To provide a process to help us (1) go inside to find our authentic selves and (2) deactivate our old, undesirable conditioning so that we may (3) retrain ourselves to fully be and express our authentic selves.*

Life Mastery begins to deactivate our *old conditioning* by helping us identify and release old habits, patterns, and attachments that keep us *stuck* in lack and limitation. It encourages us to take responsibility for creating our *new* lives and sets us on the path of true fulfillment by teaching us how to *think with our hearts.* That prepares us for the ultimate goal, which is to *identify our unique gifts, talents, and personal qualities and take them out into the world in ways that bring us joy and fulfillment.*

As we work through the lessons, *Life Mastery* gradually moves us to *new* levels of *consciousness* so that we may fully *be* and *express* who we are. We learn to create new *intentions* for our lives and to develop the clarity and courage we need to state our *needs,* speak our *truth* without intention to harm, and set our *boundaries*—necessary tools for creating healthy, balanced lives.

Ultimately, what impresses me most about this program is the sheer *authority* of the teachings. Professional therapists, counselors, and coaches are trained to help us explore our issues and improve our lives using hearty doses of *guidance* and *positive reinforcement* to bolster our courage and self-esteem. And that, of course, can be healthy and valuable. However, when the Archangel Michael counsels us to "stand in your greatness," "don't try to fit in," "blaze your own path," and "step fearlessly into the unknown," it resonates for me as powerful guidance from *God*. And that makes all the difference.

Some well-meaning friends who have participated in development workshops for this program or who have read and embraced the teachings have suggested I "hide" the spiritual source of this material because it is not *credible* in our "modern" world. In my view, it is the *source* that *gives* the program its credibility. Credibility, of course, like many things is a matter of personal discernment. As Life Mastery teaches, *use discernment to decide what is right and true for you.*

I have done so, and I am proud to proclaim to the "modern" world: *"Hey folks, this is from God. Pay attention!"*

So my counsel is that whether you are seeking a *fresh start* or wishing to set a *new course* for your life, this program will launch you on an exciting journey of *self-discovery and renewal*—if you faithfully work through the program as Archangel Michael presents it.

The more effort you put into this program, the more you will get from it. Fully engage with the process, and you will be rewarded with the expanded consciousness you need to *create the life you want and the courage to live it.*

Once you begin this new journey, you will discover that the journey never truly ends. I predict you will be changing and growing with these teachings for the rest of your life.

Bon voyage!

Joel D. Anastasi

A Message From Archangel Michael

We welcome you, as you are now ready to move into a *new* life of community, harmony, and equality.

Whether or not you know it consciously, you have reached the point where you are ready, open, and available to receive what you say you *want*.

This is not necessarily anything *outside* of you that validates or gratifies you. It is something that resonates *within* you.

Some who are reading this understand *fully* why you are here, and some of you are just getting a *glimpse* of it.

The important thing is that you are ready to find *within* you the answer to *where* you are going in the world.

As you begin the process of exploration in this program, we begin by asking:

- *Why* are you here?

- Are you here to *get* something for yourself?

- Are you here just to *get by, endure* life, and *survive?*

   Or

- Are you here to *move out into the world to express your gifts and talents?*

In your *heart* you know the answers, and it is time to take the next step.

You are here for the purpose of *world service*.

Loving who you are and what you do and bringing that out into the world is world service.

The answers to how you can do that are in your *heart*. That is why this program is designed to take you on a journey from the core of your *mind* into the core of your *heart*.

The messages and exercises contained within this program are *tools* to be utilized while making this journey.

As you begin reading the first message in lesson one, you will begin a process of allowing your *heart* to become the guiding force of your life. For some, the shift in consciousness that makes this possible is *gradual*. For others, it is *sudden*.

The process involves peeling layer upon layer of *wounding* from around your heart until you have moved *into* your heart and uncovered the essence of your *truth*. As you *release* each layer of wounding that surrounds your heart, you will also raise the level of resonance and vibration *within* you.

This occurs because each layer of wounding is filled with lower vibration energy, which simply represents what you have learned during childhood about how to *survive* in the world and how you were *conditioned*.

The intention of this program is to begin to peel away these layers of wounding.

As you progress through the lessons, you will discover your talents and gifts, and you will realize that your *purpose in life involves giving these talents and gifts to the world in ways that bring you fulfillment and joy.*

By engaging in this process of self-discovery, you will raise the level of resonance and vibration in *yourself.*

As you accomplish this, you will raise the level of resonance and vibration of the *world,* thus helping to co-create a new world of *community, harmony,* and *equality.*

How To Use This Workbook

Life Mastery is designed to be a *self-study* program. The learning is enhanced, however, when you work with others in *groups*. We encourage you to form Life Mastery groups where you can help each other process your issues, grow in consciousness, and incorporate these teachings into your lives.

This program, as we have told you, has a *divine* source. It is not a long program, but every paragraph and page contains valuable wisdom. The more you work with the material, the more wisdom you will discover, learn, and be empowered to employ.

We suggest you spend two to three hours each week completing one lesson a week for sixteen weeks. That generally is enough time to do the work the lessons require and to experience the momentum of the lessons building upon themselves. Ultimately, of course, follow a schedule that works for you. Michael urges that the lessons be done in the order they are presented.

If you are working in a group, we recommend that you come together two to three hours each week. If that is not convenient, try to meet at least twice a month to discuss how you are experiencing the teachings and exercises and how the lessons are showing up in your lives.

For those wishing to participate in a facilitated Life Mastery workshop, we at the Angel News Network plan to present Life Mastery webinars from time to time. Check for upcoming Life Mastery programs on our website: http://www.theangelnewsnetwork.com.

Get a notebook and begin to journal your experiences, responses, and thoughts as you work through the program. Journaling helps clarify your thinking and creates a record of your developing consciousness. As you review your journal, you will begin to see and understand yourself in new ways, which will provide valuable new insights for how to create the life you want and the courage to live it.

Here are some general guidelines for working together in your own peer-run groups.

1. Begin each session by allowing members to *briefly* share how the program's teachings are showing up in their lives. Then move to a discussion of the key teachings in the current lesson(s).

2. Discussions of how participants experienced the exercises are best done in small groups of three or four. Groups of two limit the feedback. Larger groups tend to become unwieldy.

3. The answers to the questions in this program lie *within* us. So we serve others best by *listening* to how they are experiencing the lessons and exercises. To keep the discussions clear and focused and to help each other explore more deeply what is "within," it occasionally can be helpful to ask clarifying questions, such as, Could you be more specific? What is an example of that? When do you plan to start? What do you think is stopping you? etc.

4. Refrain from trying to "fix" others. Briefly sharing your own *relevant* personal experiences can be useful, but don't turn someone *else's* sharing into a discussion about *you* or to try to impose your views on others.

5. Create a "safe" place by maintaining each other's *self-esteem.* This program encourages participants to explore sensitive issues, including emotional *wounding* that has kept them stuck in lack and limitation. Participants are more willing to share if they feel safe.

6. All participants should have the opportunity to share *equally.* No one should dominate the discussion. Agree on time frames for sharing.

7. Trust the *process.* The wisdom is written into the program through the lessons and exercises. Again, the answers to most of our questions lie *within* us. The keys to unlocking the answers are in the *teachings* and *exercises.*

8. This program prepares you to decide *where* you want to go in the world. Once you decide, there are plenty of career-planning and job-search

resources available in libraries, bookstores, and the Internet to help you plan strategies for achieving what you want. Use them.

9.   Have *fun*. Laugh. Lighten up. Most issues are not as serious as we make them. Life is a *process*, not a destination. Seek to make your process an *adventure*. Challenges contain important *lessons*. Always ask, what is the lesson here? When you can't think of anything else to do, smile. It tricks the brain. Remember, this is about creating *joy* in our lives!

10. When you are feeling *stuck* or need to be *refreshed*, return to Life Mastery for guidance. You will be amazed how fast your questions get answered. For a quick spiritual fix, revisit the counsel Quado and Steve Jobs offer at the beginning of this book. They're both essentially saying the same thing: *Create the life you want and the courage to live it! Go for it!*

Grounding Exercise

Complete this simple grounding exercise before beginning work on a *new* lesson or exercise. It will *shift* your consciousness and help you be more *receptive* to the learning.

Sit upright in a comfortable chair with your back supported and your feet firmly on the floor. Close your eyes and rest for a moment.

- Slowly breathe in through your nose and out through your mouth three times.

- As you breathe, move into the depth of your heart and connect with the essence of you.

- With each breath, mentally repeat: "I release and let go."

- Fully release your thoughts from your mind.

- Let go of looking for answers, and just allow yourself to *be*.

- Remain where you are as long as you need to in stillness and silence.

- When you are ready, open your eyes and begin.

Break Old Habits and Patterns That Keep You In Lack and Limitation

INTRODUCTION

You realize that significant aspects of what's *old* in your life no longer work. On your life journey, you have come to an *intersection* or perhaps the *end* of the road.

In many ways you are at the *end* of an *old* life and are looking ahead to move into a *new* life. But you are not sure what that new life *looks* like or *where* it will take you.

The new life represents your *soul's divine plan.* It is not a job or a relationship or any one thing you are supposed to do. There are many *facets* to your soul plan. They come from knowing *who* you are.

The *wounded* little girl or boy who lives *inside* you has guided your life up to this point. It is now time to move into full self-individuation from mom and dad to *release* shame and judgment.

Approach these lessons with the intention of *healing* the wounds of the *inner child.*

As an adult you may invite the child to walk hand in hand with you as you make this journey. *You guide the child.*

You will heal sufficiently to fulfill your soul purpose as long as you keep *awakening* to yourself.

1

At this intersection, before you move forward on the new road, it is time to stop and look *behind* you at *old* habits and patterns.

Moving forward requires leaving fragments of your *old* life behind—especially old *habits and patterns* that may allow you to feel "safe" or "comfortable" but keep you in lack and limitation.

EXERCISE ONE 🖎

1. Identify and write down *habits* (including ways of thinking) and *behavior patterns* that keep you in lack and limitation.

    Ask yourself:

    *   What are my specific patterns and habits that I know *limit* me?

    *   Which patterns and habits do I desperately want to *move out* of but just can't seem to?

    *   Why do I *maintain* these patterns?

You maintain these habits and patterns because they give you the illusion of being in *control* of your life. You are essentially saying to yourself: "If I follow this pattern, it is going to lead me somewhere."

    Ask yourself:

    *   Where are these patterns leading me?

Answer: to a place that is *familiar* and *comfortable*. These patterns are guiding you to places where you may *say* you don't want to be, but you are very *comfortable* being there. These patterns offer you the "comfort" of knowing where you are going because they lead you to the "security" of the *familiar*—as opposed to allowing your heart to move you into the "insecurity" of the *unknown*.

2. Once you identify what these habits and patterns are, ask:

    *   Can I *accept* where I am?

(This program is teaching you *compassion* and *acceptance* for yourself and for others. Accepting yourself with compassion *frees* you to make *new* life choices.)

3.   Once you have accepted where you are, ask:

- What do I need to *change?*

- Can I make *another* choice?

Your ego may come up with warnings, such as, "The status quo is fine. Change is risky and scary." Be with the *feelings* that come up. These feelings are in the depth of your *heart* where you find your *truth.* Emotions are feelings in *motion.* Feel your feelings, and they will move, change, and usually pass.

4.   Decide to make a *new* choice. Be with the feelings that come up. Begin to feel the feelings of taking *responsibility* for your life—that *you* are the source and creator that can change your life.

5.   Then open to a new *idea,* a new *thought,* and a new *vision* simply by making a new *choice.*

Accept the feelings that come up when you make a decision to *change* your old patterns and adopt new behaviors. Your feelings will help you understand why you remain in and continue the old patterns and why you have been committed to them.

You are now breaking a *lineage* of *past* customs and patterns handed down to you by your parents, their parents, and their parents' parents. You are making a choice to energetically *cut* those links. You will begin to feel *energetic shifts* within your body as you begin to break the lineage.

Those old habits and patterns influence the life that you live *now* and will influence your *future* unless you identify them for what they are and make a choice to break that chain.

EXERCISE TWO 🖎

Meditate on the answers you have given in exercise one. Listen to what you hear, not with your mind but with your *heart.* Allow yourself to feel, to see, to hear, and to trust that you can move into the *unknown*—the unknown being in the depth of your heart. As you meditate, ask:

1. What habits and patterns (routines) do I repeat every day that I find *comfortable* and *familiar* that lead me to a place of lack and limitation as opposed to a place of *self-expression, abundance,* and *prosperity?*

2. Which habits and patterns need to be *broken?*

3. What do I need to do to *change* them?

4. *Visualize* yourself making the choice to *change* the habit or pattern without concerning yourself about the *result.* (In this program, let go of thinking about results.)

This process teaches you to be in the *moment* of the *unknown* where the wounded inner child looks out on the road of *possibility* called the *unknown—where creation takes place.*

Remember, making this change will begin to *break* a lineage passed down from your biological family and your culture. You will be creating a resonance and a vibration of energy that will allow the *macrocosm* to break its chain and its lineage. You will be, in effect, telling the universe: *That pattern ends here!*

This is where you begin to take *responsibility* for creating the life you want.

SUMMARY

This program prepares you for *world service* by moving you fully into your heart—your *inner truth*. Release the *mind,* the thought process of the *ego.* Fully immerse yourself in the depth of your *heart.*

Listen to what you hear, what you see, and what you feel, not with your mind but with your heart. Begin to trust, to move into the unknown, into your heart.

This lesson is the first step in helping you shift *old* habits and patterns and *release* the energy of the *old* way of life, which no longer *resonates* for you.

Continue to observe *where* you are as you lead yourself toward what you say you *want.* Answer these questions to assess where you are at any moment.

- Who am I?

- What am I feeling?

- Where am I in the moment?

- How well do I know myself in this moment?

- How am I feeling about my life now?

- Where is my sense of self?

- Where is my power?

- Where am I still looking outside of me for *others* to define who I am?

- Where do I think of myself as powerless or not good enough?

- Where am I still hiding?

Your answers will *change* as you move through the program.

Release Attachments That Do Not Serve Your Highest Good

INTRODUCTION

You are here to learn to tap into the power *within,* the power of *creation.*

Creation is about creating the *new*—that which has *never been.*

You are experiencing a master *shift.* You are opening your heart to navigate that passageway into your *inner truth*—to be able to love, feel, express, and embody the depth of your truth.

This program allows the *transmutation* of old patterns—whereby you examine your *old* patterns and, if you choose, change them in a *positive* way.

You are looking to move from a place of *limitation* to a place of *power.*

You are looking to free yourself from *attachments* outside yourself that have *limited* you and to harness your power of self-expression to bring your *gifts* and *talents* into the world.

I. IDENTIFY YOUR ATTACHMENTS

It is important to identify your *attachments* outside of yourself, which may offer some level of gratification or comfort but are keeping you in lack and limitation.

Notice how you use your attachments to look outside of yourself for *validation* and *permission* to express your truth.

EXERCISE ONE 🖎❚

Look *outside* of yourself to see the mirrors (people and circumstances) that will *show* you your attachments.

1. Ask and write down:

    *   What am I attached to *outside* of myself (people, places, things)?

    *   What do the attachments outside of myself *represent* to me?

    *   What do my attachments allow me to *do* or *not* do?

    *   How do my attachments bring me *validation* and *gratification*?

    *   Are any of my attachments really *addictions*?

    *   How do my attachments help or hinder my *ability to be me*?

    *   Which attachments *stifle* my voice? (Usually relates to family.)

2. What do I need to *change*?

    *   Whether or not I decide to change, what issues will I still be *avoiding*?

3. *Decide* what you need to change.

    *   Your ability to *release* and *let go* will reveal your power to fully *individuate*.

- When you begin to look at and understand your specific attachments, strong feelings may come up as you recall specific situations in which you have *not* stated your *needs,* expressed your *truth,* or set your *boundaries.*

Identify these situations and have the feelings.

This may be a time of letting go and cutting cords, including *relationships* with some wonderful people who *no longer serve your highest good.*

Ultimately, this is about *your* highest good, which will translate into the highest good for *all.*

II. BEING ALONE

You may be tested with deep feelings, including the *fear* of being alone.

Many of you have *never* been alone.

Many do not *understand* what truly being alone is.

Being truly alone involves life mastery—fully standing alone, fully making that choice, fully letting go of the *attachments* to what is *outside* of you.

The willingness to completely stand alone is an important step in fully taking *responsibility* for your own life.

Identifying and seeing your attachments will reveal to you how you *resist* being alone and may trigger core feelings and wounds.

EXERCISE TWO 🖎▌

1. Spontaneously, from your heart, write down your *definition* of alone.

    (To connect with the *authentic* you and create a *new* path for your life, you must be willing to stand alone, individuated, honoring and valuing who you are.)

    Your definition may surprise you.

2. Ask yourself:

    •   What does being alone *mean* to me?

    •   Can I *be* alone?

    •   Do I *enjoy* being alone?

    •   Am I *giving* what I need to myself?

    •   Am I looking *outside* myself to get what I think I lack?

    •   Can I stand alone, loving, honoring, and *giving to myself*?

3. During this next week, be alone with you as much as you can. You will begin to find out what it is like to be truly alone. Many of you have *negative* connotations about being alone:

    •   "I have been fighting the feeling of being alone all my life."

    •   "Alone is bad."

    •   "Alone means I am not liked or loved."

Be with the feelings that come up for you and write them down.

4. The experience of being alone will help you begin to assess your relationship with *yourself* and how that affects your relationships with *others*. Record in your journal your experience of being alone and your answers to these questions:

    •   Am *I* giving what I need to myself? Or am I looking *outside* myself to get what I think is not within me?

    •   What could I *give* to myself that would allow me to stand alone, loving, honoring, and giving to myself?

SUMMARY

This lesson challenges you to identify where drama pervades your life with attachments that do *not* serve your highest good—how putting situations and people on *pedestals* challenges your sense of equality and compromises your ability to identify, develop, and use your unique gifts and talents. Ask yourself:

- Do I see myself as *equal,* or do I look to *others* to determine my truth?

- Am I ready to move to a place of *equality* and *power* and to exercise that power for my full *self-expression?*

Picture a staircase. You are at the bottom of this staircase. Each lesson in this program as you complete the exercises (which help you look at your life) is another step *up* that staircase.

You are ascending into life mastery. You are ascending to your *place* in the world and integrating yourself into your *new* life.

You are beginning to tap into the power *within,* the power of *creation.*

Shift Your Focus to the Inner Self as the Creator

INTRODUCTION

You are moving into *self-realization* as you are guided to the opening of your *soul's divine plan.*

The *mirrors* of life are being shown to you so you may see *where* you are, what your *commitments* are, and what reality you are *choosing* for yourself.

As you look at the mirrors, you are realizing that you have *not* accepted your *feelings.* In fact, you have been committed to *avoiding* them through the choices you have made (playing it safe, avoiding rejection or anger of others, risk of failure, ignoring feelings of dissatisfaction, etc.)

This has allowed you to remain in lack and limitation and comfort zones that do *not* support your highest good.

Consequently you have felt dissatisfied and unfulfilled—signs of the *unrealized* self.

So we ask, has your life been shaped primarily by:

- Factors *outside* of yourself (pressures and judgments of parents, authority figures, culture, etc.)?

  Or

- Priorities of your *heart* (your *inner* self)?

EXERCISE ONE ✍

1. Over the next week, continue to examine your habits, patterns, and attachments, and notice which *stand out*.

2. To which of the following do your habits, patterns, and attachments apply:

    *   Are you committed to *avoiding* your feelings and staying in your *comfort zones* and in lack and limitation? For example, are you avoiding what you *resonate* with because it may appear impractical, you lack experience, you're not good enough, you fear rejection, etc.?

        Or

    *   Are you committed to moving toward what you say you *want*, what *resonates* in your *heart*, the path toward life mastery?

    Many feelings may come up that you have always tried to *avoid*: fear, sadness, anger, etc. Accept your feelings with compassion.

3. Write down:

    *   Which habits, patterns, and attachments need to be *changed?*

    *   The *choices* you have before you. See how you can *simplify* and how you can *change* what needs to be changed.

Notice that most, if not all, of your habits patterns and attachments (including your fears) cause you to focus on things *outside* of yourself.

It is time now to take that attention from *outside* and move it *within* so that you may begin to take *responsibility* for you and make *choices* that reflect your truth.

Let go of *blaming* outside factors for your feelings or the conditions of your life. They just reflect your *choices*.

EXERCISE TWO 🖎

You are learning there is a *power* brewing *inside* you—the desire for *self-expression.* There is power in your *voice* and your *word,* and you want to express *all* of you.

You have something to say, something to offer, and you are strong enough to stop focusing your attention "out there" and to *change* your patterns and attachments that keep you in lack and limitation.

It is time to explore the *unrealized* self.

1. Ask and write down:

    *   What is *important* to me?

    *   What have I *not* expressed within myself that I would like to express *now?*

    *   What *gifts and talents* do I have that can help me express my unrealized self?

Accept your feelings and have compassion for what is *revealed* to you so you can understand that you have *choices.*

By taking responsibility for yourself, you are tapping into your power, the power of one, the power of the *I AM. I AM* in charge. *I AM* the creator. *I AM* the source.

2. Over the next week, focus on the *inner* self as the creator.

    Acknowledge what has been revealed to you, and share your revelations and feelings with your group.

    You are now fully acknowledging the *commitment* you are making to *you.*

SUMMARY

As you do these exercises, you are beginning to realize that what you have made so important is *not* so important. Your *old* behaviors were simply holding you in a place of lack and limitation where attachments, habits, and patterns are concerned.

You are beginning to understand that they reflect the attention you place outside of yourself. They are not as important as moving toward life mastery, which involves looking *inside yourself to bring your gifts and talents out into the world in ways that brings you joy and fulfillment.*

Like it or not, by making this commitment to *you* during this program, all the feelings you have been trying to avoid are coming to the surface for you now.

Many of you are beginning to feel feelings you have *never* felt before because these were the feelings you feared enough to resist or avoid.

That is a sign that you are *shifting* your attention and commitment from things that helped you avoid your feelings to the *unrealized* self in the depth of your heart.

Accept and assimilate your feelings and have *compassion* for yourself.

You are fine-tuning and simplifying the ways in which you are moving toward life mastery.

Develop Discernment to Make Choices That Serve Your Highest Good and the Highest Good of All

INTRODUCTION

Your confidence is growing in your ability to make your *own* decisions.

You are becoming more conscious of your behavior *patterns* and *attachments* and how they have influenced your choices.

You are now ready to *release* them.

Instead of repeating past behavior patterns, you are recognizing that you have many choices available to you. You are now ready to make *different* choices based on *discernment*.

Discernment involves consciously connecting with your senses to discern what is true for you—what resonates for you as it relates to your choices and decisions and what does not.

As your *consciousness* shifts, what *resonates* for you will shift and change as well. That is why it is important before acting or responding to a situation to:

- Take a moment to *center* yourself (breathe).

- Enter into *neutrality* (release achieving a particular outcome).

- Ask appropriate *questions*(What are my *feelings* telling me? What do I *resonate* with? What message am I getting from my *heart?* etc.)

EXERCISE ONE: DEVELOPING DISCERNMENT 🖎◗

Developing discernment requires developing the ability to be *receptive—* to be *present* in your physical body, so that you can be open to the *guidance* you receive from your *senses,* your *feelings,* and your *heart.*

- Relax your body and *breathe* (See grounding exercise).

- Mentally scan your body and notice any tension, tightness, or constriction. Allow it to be.

- Visualize a pulsating, golden light gradually expanding from your heart until it fills your whole body.

- Ask your *heart* about the question/issue for which you are seeking discernment.

- Ask your *body,* Does the response *resonate* with me, or does it *not* resonate with me?

- *Feel* your body's response:

    - Positive: a feeling of expansion, lightness, clarity, comfort, and resonance.

    - Negative: a feeling of tightness or contraction, discomfort, or dissonance.

As you practice this technique, you will increasingly pay attention to your *senses*–what your feelings and your heart are telling you. You will gradually build confidence in your ability to discern.

EXERCISE TWO: PRACTICING DISCERNMENT ✍

How do you discern when you are confronted with many *choices*?

The key is to feel your *feelings*, get in touch with your *senses*, let go of any attachment to a particular *outcome*, and decide what you *resonate* with.

1. Consider some *new* choices for a *change* you have decided to make. Feel your feelings and ask:

    *   Do I have total *freedom* to make this choice? (Or am I still attached to a particular *outcome*, concerned about what others think, stuck in my head, etc.)

    *   Have I recognized and *freed* myself from repeating past patterns and attachments?

If you can honor and recognize these factors, you are now at a level of consciousness where you can take *responsibility* for your choices.

2. As you take full responsibility for your *new* choices, ask yourself:

    *   Which choice is the choice of my *mind*?

    *   Which choice resonates in my *heart*?

    *   Which choice offers the greatest *opportunity* to use my gifts and talents in a *joyful* way?

    *   Which choice is most likely to make me feel *joyful* and *fulfilled*?

3. Use your tools, breathe, and be willing to be in the confusion or chaos until discernment arrives. With the clarity of discernment, you will *feel* and *be* empowered.

Learning to discern and to choose what truly *resonates* for you is the best way to serve your highest good and the highest good of all.

SUMMARY

The further you progress in this program, the more we will be challenging your *conditioning*.

Repeatedly, we will be asking you to pay attention to your *heart*, your *intuition*, and what *resonates* for you.

When you are connected to your *heart*, paying attention to your *intuition* and to what *resonates* for you, you will be using discernment to create the life path that is *right* for you.

Think with Your Heart

(A review of what we have covered and a look at where we are headed.)

I. PROGRAM REVIEW

What You Have Learned

These lectures and exercises have begun to *empower* some of you and have, to some degree, *frightened* others of you.

Some are looking to open a window and *fly,* while others are afraid of their new exposure and want to move back into a "safe" cocoon.

Either way, you're discovering that there is no going back, because that "safe" place is no longer available to you. It no longer *resonates* for you.

You have moved to a *new* level of consciousness because you have realized how you have suppressed your unique *voice* and freedom of *expression* through your habits, patterns, attachments, what you have made important, and where you have put your focus.

You are finding a *new* power within. You are beginning to:

- *Express* yourself in *new* ways.

- Open to *receive* love, especially from yourself.

- Open to *give* love without attachment.

- Discover that it is OK to *be* you with all your feelings.

- *Release* feelings of judgment and shame.

• Make choices that *resonate* for you.

EXERCISE ONE

This is a good time to assess what you have experienced in the past few weeks as you have taken your *new* consciousness out into your world. Write your answers in your journal.

1. First, examine your relationship with *yourself.*

    • What have you *learned* about yourself? Any surprises?

    • How has your relationship with yourself *changed?*

    • What were your most important *experiences?*

    • What is the most profound *aspect* that you learned about you?

2. Now examine your relationships with *others.*

    • What have you learned about your *relationships* (patterns, attachments)?

    • How have your relationships with others *changed?*

    • Which of your relationships have a *balance* of *giving* and *receiving?*

    • Which relationships do *not* have that balance?

3. Examine how you make *choices.*

    • What *new* consciousness have you brought to making choices?

    • How has the influence of *others* in your decision-making process *changed?*

4. Summing up:

    • Where have you *grown?*

- What about you is *changing?*

Look at the glass as half *full* rather than half empty.

Move to a place of *abundance*. Focus on what you *have* done, not what you have not. Acknowledge where you need to grow, but focus on *where* you have used the tools, knowledge, and lessons you have learned.

II. THINK WITH YOUR HEART

What Is Ahead

During the rest of this program, we are going to focus on where there is *love* in your life, especially your love for *yourself* and what you love and resonate with in the *world*.

Your love for yourself powers your courage to be you!

That is why we are teaching you to move spontaneously from your *mind* (where the influences of the *world* reside) to your *heart* (where your *truth* and *true* path lie.)

Ultimately, you are being taught to *think with your heart*. When you can think with your heart, you are no longer ruled by the conditioning and influence of *others*.

You begin to create your life with what resonates in your heart.

Your mind is filled with echoes of judgments from mom and dad, teachers, authority figures, etc. who *conditioned* you to believe you were unlovable, incompetent, not good enough, not smart or mature enough to make your own choices, etc. Those judgments have *nothing* to do with truth or reality—unless you let them.

What is real and true for you is in the depth of your *heart*.

That is why we are teaching you to move spontaneously from your mind to your heart—*to think with your heart*.

We are *not* suggesting that the mind does not have value. On the contrary, it is essential. *For the mind can create what the heart knows.*

In that way the mind becomes a *servant* of the heart. That is what it means to think with the heart.

The exercises in future lessons will help you explore the truth that lies in your *heart.*

EXERCISE TWO 🖎

You are ready to connect with your *inner* self. Therefore, we ask you to:

- Write down where *negative* thoughts, memories, and judgments hold you back to the point where the development and expression of your gifts and talents may be significantly *compromised.*

- Identify what you *shame* and *judge* about you (not good enough, etc.).

- Be aware of these behavior patterns when you begin to feel *anxious or fearful* about making choices and taking actions that resonate for you.

- Replace these thoughts by acknowledging and writing down examples of your *worthiness,* your *accomplishments,* and the *strides* you have taken to be where you are now.

EXERCISE THREE 🖎

Without thinking about it, spontaneously write down your definition of *love.* When writing this definition, where do you spontaneously go— to your mind or to your *heart?*

You have been conditioned to think with your mind. We are teaching you to think with your heart. Begin by paying attention to the *spontaneity* of where you are at every moment. Do you go where you were *taught* (your mind) or to a place of *intuition,* of love, in your heart? In essence, do you revert to your *old* patterns and attachments or move to the *new?*

This is *confusing* for many of you. Your reference point of looking *outside* of yourself (the old) is beginning to wane and you are looking for a *new* reference point. What can you trust? Who can you trust?

This program is preparing you to love and trust *you.*

As you raise your awareness of your *self-love,* you will recognize and encounter *love* more and more in your relationships and in the world.

III. RECLAIMING YOURSELF

Those of you who are committing to this program are committing to the *glorification,* the *embodiment* and the *full expression* of you.

You are, in effect, *reclaiming* yourself.

That is why you have chosen to participate in these teachings—*to rediscover your greatness and power in order to consciously create the life you want.*

GUIDING PRINCIPLES FOR CONSCIOUSLY CREATING YOUR LIFE

- Focus on your *progress* and *accomplishments.*

- Acknowledge your *challenges* without dramatizing them (I'm stuck in this hopeless job, relationship, etc.), and look for the *lessons* they contain.

- Use your tools. Ask:

   - What are my *patterns* and *attachments* here?

   - Have I *freed* myself to choose what serves my highest good and the good of others?

   - Where am I *focusing* my attention (glass half empty or half filled, etc.)?

- What am I *shaming* and *judging?*

- Am I giving and receiving in *balance?*

- What *resonates* for me?

- What is my *intuition* telling me?

- How will this choice serve *my* highest good and the highest good of *others?*

- Which of my gifts and talents will I be able to use in *joyful* ways?

By thoroughly exploring these questions and following the guidance in this program, you will reach the point where you can state:

"I am fully, consciously creating my life."

That is how you reclaim yourself.

EXERCISE FOUR

1. Find a quiet, soothing area of your home. Read this entire lesson *three* times and absorb it.

   While reading, imagine a golden-white light cascading down upon you, and think of it as a warm energetic white blanket. Wrap yourself in this energetic light blanket and imagine it as your *soul support system.*

2. After the third reading, reflect on where you have given yourself the freedom, the choice, and the power to *fly* in life, to let go of all the stops, to let go of all your limitations, to open to the depth and breadth of you.

   Allow it to penetrate. Write down immediately what you *feel* and what comes to you spontaneously.

3. Then put your notes away. Go back in twenty-four hours and read what you have written. Add or change whatever your *heart* suggests.

SUMMARY

Focusing on success and abundance creates a *consciousness* of success and abundance.

- Focus on what *is* there (glass half full, your accomplishments), *not* on what you *lack* (glass half empty) and what you still need to work on or *fix*.

- Focus on what is *working* for you, what is *in* your life, where there is *abundance,* and how to retrain yourself to *be* in that place. Look at where there is *ease* in your life.

- Notice and consider how to change or let go of where you *struggle.*

- Challenges will always be with you. They can be sources of *learning.* Begin to integrate challenges into your life in *balance* with your accomplishments, so you no longer view challenges simply as negatives that you need to get *rid of* or *fix*.

Are you beginning to trust that you have the ability and the power to *create* the life you want?

Harness the Power of Intention and of the Word

INTRODUCTION

You have arrived at a place of power in your *heart*.

You are beginning to look down the road of *possibilities* connected to your *wonder child,* some with more confidence than others. (Your wonder child looks forward to the exciting adventures and opportunities that life offers.)

Still, you are tapping into a place called *knowingness*—knowing *who* and *where* you are and where you would *like* to be.

By being conscious and in charge of your life, you are on the path to connecting to your *inner truth,* your *soul plan*.

It is time to begin creating *intentions* for your life.

I. THE POWER OF INTENTION

An intention is a statement of how you intend to freely give your talents and gifts to the world without attachment—letting them go into the universe by simply stating, "These are my intentions."

Intentions put you in the director's chair from which you may *direct* your own life.

By *announcing* your intentions, you are fully declaring yourself in the world, individualized, self-contained, and standing in your power, stating:

"Here I am. This is what I honor and value about me. This is what I choose to give and to achieve."

You are connecting with your *intuition* and are moving through your heart toward trusting you—trusting that you can leap off the mountain and *fly*.

Trust that you can create intentions for yourself that will *guide* you as you move toward what you say you *want*.

EXERCISE ONE

Move into a meditative state, into your *heart*, to a place of solitude and quiet. Write down what you are hearing with your *heart* as you do this exercise. If possible, do this in dim light or candlelight so you can see what you are writing.

1. Listening to your heart, list five to ten *intentions* for your life.

2. As you make your list, consider these thoughts and questions:

    *   What is *important* to me?

    *   What *gifts* and *talents* do I intend to give to the world that I will use to create abundance and prosperity?

    *   Where do I see myself *giving, loving,* and experiencing *joy*?

    *   Write from a place of the glass is *full*, not from what needs to be *fixed*.

    *   Be in a place of *now*, looking toward *how* you wish to express yourself as you *create* the life you want. (Let go of thinking about results.)

    *   As you write your intentions, look down the road of *possibility*, seeing all the wonderful *aspects* of life you wish to partake in.

You are building momentum as you gather knowledge and remember all of the unclaimed aspects of you. Firmly ground yourself by breathing deeply.

We will revisit your intentions throughout this program.

II. THE POWER OF THE WORD

Words have the power to *create* or to *destroy*.

Your word can send *vibrations* of love, joy, encouragement, strength, success, abundance, friendship, and more to lift your resonance and the resonance of others. Your word has the power to *manifest* your intentions and *create* a world of community, harmony, and equality. Your word also has the power to *dissolve* the *fear* that can trap you and others in lack and limitation.

Your word can also do *damage* to you and to others. Therefore, when you express yourself, pay attention to the *effect* of your word and how it is *received*. Observe your power—to help, guide, and teach for the good of a changing world into which you have chosen to bring your talents and gifts.

III. IMPECCABILITY OF THE WORD

Impeccability means being *without sin*. Sin means "off the mark" and is anything you do that seeks to harm you or another. So impeccability of your word means to *not* use your word a*gainst* yourself or another.

Many of you think impeccability of the word refers only to the way you speak to someone *else*. It also refers to how you communicate with *yourself*. Remember, your word has the power to *create* or to *destroy*.

EXERCISE TWO 🖎

Pay attention to *how* you communicate with *yourself* and *others*. Write your answers to the following questions in your journal:

- What have you been *telling* you about you?

- Have you been *listening* to and *acknowledging* yourself and others?

- Have you been *loving, honoring, and encouraging* yourself and others?

- Have you been using your word to *create or to destroy*?

- How do you intend to use the power of the word to help *achieve* your intentions?

IV. COMPASSION

As you move through each lesson, you rise to another level of *compassion*—for yourself and for others. You now feel compassion for where you are in life and for the *wounding* of others.

You are seeing all this with a power that can make a difference and bring about *change*.

Without compassion, change *cannot* occur, because you will remain in a place of *separation* where it is me *against* them.

That is why we ask you to pay attention when expressing yourself. Are your words creating *unity* or *separation*?

Once you become conscious of the effect of your word, you will develop the consciousness of *compassion* that is needed to create a new world of community, harmony, and equality.

SUMMARY

1. You are now claiming parts of you that you have *never* claimed before, because you are now *choosing* your life.

2. Survey the realm of *possibility* for your life while holding firmly to your intentions, and ask yourself:

   - What is most *important* to me?

   - Where can I *give* my gifts and talents in a way that brings me *joy?*

3. Finally, ask yourself to which are you committed:

   - To indulging in what is *familiar* and *comfortable*—stuck in the illusion that you have *no* choices in life, where everything *outside* of you dictates your life?

     Or

   - To changing, growing, prospering, and giving and receiving in service to the world?

If the latter, then fully *immerse* yourself in your intentions.

Your intentions are you.

Take Responsibility for Yourself

INTRODUCTION

This program is designed to *empower* you by teaching you to take *responsibility* for yourself.

The ultimate goal of this program is to prepare you to take your *place* in the world (bringing your gifts and talents into the world) by enabling you to come from a place of power *inside* as opposed to you looking *outside* of yourself for validation and approval.

I. EVALUATE YOUR INTENTIONS

EXERCISE ONE

1. Look at the *intentions* you wrote in lesson six, and notice whether your focus was *inside* you or *outside.*

    Ask yourself:

    *   Am I still looking *outside* of myself for others to define for me who I am and where I should be, so I can stay in the *familiar* and feel *safe?*

        Or

- Am I looking at the realm of *possibility,* the *unknown,* knowing that I am the *source* and the *creator* and therefore taking *responsibility* for creating the life I say I want?

2. Are your intentions written with the intention and need to get something *back?*

- Your intentions are not a fishing line that you throw out hoping something bites that you can *pull back in.*

- Intentions are based on what you *honor* and *value* about yourself, giving your gifts freely without attachment and letting them go into the universe, simply saying, "These are my intentions." Let them go into the universe, *trusting* they will be created exactly as they should within your soul's divine plan.

II. TRUST YOURSELF

When you know yourself as the *creator,* every moment becomes a moment of *creation.* Every moment presents an opportunity for you to declare to the world *who* you are. You are learning to trust yourself enough to be able to declare and tell the world:

- *Here* I am.

- This is what I *honor* and *value* about me.

- I no longer need to go *outside* of myself for validation, gratification, or confirmation.

- I am fully contained and fulfilled *within* me.

- This is what I choose to *give.*

Trust is *not* blind faith. Simply stating, "I will open up to the energies and powers of the universe and trust that I will be safe and secure" will *not* place you in a state of trust.

In order to develop trust in yourself, you must take full responsibility for you.

EXERCISE TWO 🖎

Ask yourself:

- Where am I taking full *responsibility* for myself and where am I *not?*

- Where am I looking *outside* of myself at the mirror and taking responsibility for *my* part in what the mirror is showing me?

It is important to take responsibility for *where* you are in the moment and *what* the mirror is showing you.

III. FOCUS ON YOUR ACCOMPLISHMENTS

A good place to start building trust in yourself is to look at what you have *accomplished* in your life—in other words, where you are *now* in relation to where you *began.*

EXERCISE THREE 🖎

1. Answer and list the following:

    - What have I *accomplished* in my life?

    - What *positive occurrences* allowed me to move to where I am now?

    - What *choices* have I made that have brought me to this place?

2. Review your answers to encode in your *cellular structure* how your *accomplishments* have brought you to this moment—as opposed to figuring out how you need to *improve* or *fix* yourself.

    Many of you feel that you are not good enough—yet. You have not accomplished enough—yet.

    Many of you believe you must make a never-ending effort to accomplish *more,* to move toward something—though you're not sure what that is. A major reason for this is that you have not fully realized and accepted your *accomplishments* and truly *received* them.

3. Your list of accomplishments should be *endless*. Add to your list every day, if possible.

4. Read your accomplishments. See them and allow yourself to be *in* them. Allow your feelings to come up. Take note of what you *have* done, what you are *grateful* for, and what is *important* to you.

IV. ASSESS YOUR PRIORITIES

You are discovering that what is important to you is *changing*.

You are realizing that a good deal of what was important to you satisfied *addictions, attachments,* and other aspects of the *wounded* self.

EXERCISE FOUR ✍

1. How have your *priorities* changed?

2. In the light of these changes, look at the meaning, value, and purpose of each of your *intentions*.

3. How have *changes* in your *priorities* affected your *intentions*? You may decide to shorten your list of intentions.

V. ASSESS YOUR RELATIONSHIPS

Your relationships provide a wonderful *mirror* for reflecting back to you the relationship you are having with *yourself*. (Example: If you don't honor and respect yourself, don't be surprised if those with whom you are in relationship don't honor and respect you either.)

All your relationships are reflections of the relationship you are having with yourself.

EXERCISE FIVE

For your *significant* relationships, ask yourself these questions and write down what comes to you:

- *What* is the relationship?

- *Why* am I having this relationship?

- What am I *relating* to?

- Are my *needs* being met?

- Is there *meaning, value,* and *purpose* in this relationship?

- Is this relationship serving my *highest good?*

- Is there a *balance* of giving and receiving in the relationship?

- How does this relationship mirror the *relationship* I am having with *myself?*

Many of your relationships are mirroring back to you the *wonderful* relationship you are having with yourself.

Some relationships will mirror *aspects* of your relationship with yourself that you would like to *shift* and *change.*

Many of you will find that you may need to *release* some of your relationships because they are *not* serving your highest good. They are not in *resonance* with the life you are *creating* for yourself.

Some relationships are allowing you to remain in a *comfort zone* of lack and limitation.

That is what you may be using the relationship for.

VI. TAKE RESPONSIBILITY FOR YOURSELF

Taking responsibility for yourself usually requires making *different* decisions and choices than you have in the past.

This can be *daunting* because to a considerable degree, your life up to now has been about satisfying the inner *wounded child.*

You are in a place of transition as you move from the *old* to the *new.*

Many of you are wondering, Can I do this? Am I good enough? Will I be safe? Will my needs be met?

Where will you look for the answers, inside or outside?

Who will provide your answers, your adult or your wounded child?

VII. TRUST YOUR SUPPORT GROUP

As you are working with the exercises and are gaining greater insights about your patterns, attachments, behaviors, and relationships, many of you are moving through deep *shame* and *judgment.* That is triggering a depth of *wounding* within you. That is why we ask you to fully *feel* your feelings.

You are seeing your *old* patterns and behaviors that perpetrated myths about you that caused you to look *outside* of yourself for validation and approval. You are now ready to *release* them.

You are also creating *intimacy* with yourself. As you do so, you increasingly desire intimacy and support from others. Therefore, it is time to trust your *support group* (if you are attending this program in a group) and use this group to share the depth and breadth of you. As you train yourself to trust *you,* you also are allowing yourself to trust your *support group.*

Use your group to move onto the road of trust. Trust an *individual* in your group with whom you can share the depth of you and know that you are still *loved.*

If you are not working with a group, ask for support from *like-minded individuals* who are on the pathway to create a new world of community, harmony, and equality.

SUMMARY

Your patterns and behaviors are so entrenched in your *nervous system* that you may feel deep *fear* when you start to let go of them.

This program is about releasing what no longer serves you and standing in your power to choose what does. As you release, you close one door and open another.

You are not sure what is on the other side of that door, and when you peek around the corner, there is *nothing* there.

However, what will be there when you walk through that doorway will be *you.*

You are moving to a place *within* you like the four- or five-year-old child who is beginning to stand up and walk on his or her own.

Stand up and open that curtain to the pathway that you once thought dark but now is *lit.*

Move into the realm of *possibility* where you can now claim:

- Your *talents* and *gifts* and what you *honor* and *value* about you.

- *How* you intend to *give* your talents and gifts to the world.

- That you are *good* enough, *powerful* enough, *perfect* and *safe* where you are with who you are.

Now stand in a place of self-acceptance and compassion as you take responsibility for your self and your life.

Trust Yourself

INTRODUCTION

The lectures and exercises in this program have taken you deeper into your *heart,* a *safe* resting place where you can build *trust* in *yourself.* You have been building trust in yourself as you have

- generated your list of *accomplishments*;

- focused on the glass half *full*—what you *have* rather than what you *don't* have; and

- stopped looking *outside* yourself for *others* to define who you are and what you should be doing with your life.

I. HONOR AND VALUE YOU

Building trust in yourself requires that you *honor* and *value* you. So we ask you:

- How do you *feel* about you?

- What do you *honor* and *value* about you?

- What is it about your *gifts* and *talents* that have meaning and value?

- What do you *do* to love you, to give support to your highest good?

- What are you *giving* to you so you can *be* you?

- What keeps you looking *outside* of you for validation and gratification?

Many of you are still looking *outside* of yourselves for confirmation that who you *are* and what you are *doing* are acceptable and worthwhile.

EXERCISE ONE 🖎▌

Mirror Exercise

Part One

The mirror exercise reveals *deeper aspects* of who you are. As you look at your reflection, thoughts and feelings may surface revealing how you have been *conditioned*.

Close your eyes. Imagine walking down a pathway into your *heart* and resting comfortably in you. When you get to this place, breathe deeply three times as follows:

Hold the breath for five seconds.

Release the breath through the throat and mouth with the strong sound of *ahhhhh*.

After the third time, become fully present, open your eyes, and do the following mirror exercise:

Part Two

The mirror exercise is best done in the *nude*. Do this exercise several times during the next week.

1. Stand *naked* in front of a mirror. Look directly into your eyes for five seconds. Then spend several seconds scanning your body from head to toe. Repeat the breathing exercise.

- Looking in your eyes, ask:

- *Who* am I?

- What am I *feeling* at this moment?

- What is it about me that I *love?*

- What is it about me that I am still *shaming* and *judging?*

- Can I *accept* my feelings and have *compassion* for myself?

- Am I ready to live my life for *me?*

2. At the end of this exercise, write down what you *feel* when you look at yourself in the mirror naked.

   - Many of you may react to this exercise with *fear.*

   - Many of you may respond with *shame* and *judgment.*

   - Others of you may *enjoy* looking at yourselves.

   - *Be* with the feelings that come up.

3. Each day after you do this exercise, write down what you *shame* and *judge* about yourself and how you feel about it. Make a separate list.

   Ask:

   - *Who* is judging and shaming me?

   - Who is *not* seeing my divine essence?

   - Can I *accept* where I am and where I shame and judge myself?

4. Negative thoughts that shame and judge you are products of your *conditioning,* what you have been *taught.* Consider your answers to the above questions. Then ask:

- *Whose* voices are these?

- What did they *teach* me?

- Do these teachings *resonate* for me now?

- Can I accept with compassion *where* I am in this moment?

- How has my *conditioning* influenced the relationship I am having with my *self*?

- How has my relationship with my *self* influenced my relationships with *others*?

It is important to use the mirror exercise whenever you *shame* or *judge* yourself. It will help you move away from the influences of negative *conditioning* and will be the jumping-off point for moving toward the life you say you want.

Part Three

The mirror exercise helps you move to new depths of intimacy *within* so that you can begin to receive love from *yourself.*

A good place to begin *receiving* love from yourself is to begin *giving* love to your inner wounded child.

- Close your eyes, move into your *heart,* and imagine your *inner wounded child.*

- When the child comes to you, look in the child's *eyes* for a few moments and be with your *feelings.*

- Ask your inner child, "What do you need in this moment?"

- After the child answers, ask yourself, "Do I love this child enough to give the child what it needs in this moment?"

- This is your opportunity to begin healing your inner child by giving *you* the love your inner child needs.

- Begin to give and receive love from *you*.

At your next group sharing, share your experience with the mirror exercise, *what* you learned, and how the experience made you *feel.*

We are leading you to trust that:

- You, fully exposed, are *good enough* just the way you are.

- The answers to what you need are *inside* you. Begin giving to *yourself* what you *need.*

II. RELEASE FEAR

Your fear may be so great that it feels "safer" for you to stay in a place that is *comfortable* rather than to feel the feelings that would be generated by moving toward *abundance, prosperity, success,* and *fulfillment.*

Fear occurs in the *absence* of love.

Remember: Your love for yourself powers your courage to be you.

EXERCISE TWO

1. List your five greatest *fears.*

   In order to write your fears, you have to be willing to *acknowledge* them. There is a fear of actually acknowledging fear.

   If this applies to you, *feel* your feelings and list them anyway.

2. Ask yourself: How are my fears affecting my ability to move *toward* what I say I want?

3. Look at your fears and ask yourself:

- Am I allowing what is *outside* of myself, including my fears, to direct my life?

  Or

- Do I love myself enough to stand in a place of *power* and direct my life with what is *important* to me?

4. How do you intend to *address* your fears?

EXERCISE THREE 📝

You have reached the *halfway* point of this program. We now ask you to *revisit* the questions you answered at the end of the lesson one, so that you may *compare* your answers and monitor your *progress* in this program.

Ask yourself:

- Who am I?

- What am I feeling?

- Where am I in this moment?

- How well do I know myself in this moment?

- How am I feeling about my life now?

- Where is my sense of self?

- Where is my power?

- Where am I looking *outside* of me for *others* to define who I am?

- Where do I think of myself as *powerless* or *not good enough?*

- Where am I still *hiding?*

We ask you to be completely truthful with that wonderful soul who is standing naked in the mirror in all of your glorious truth.

How have your answers *changed* since lesson one?

What do the changes tell you about how your consciousness has *shifted* during this program?

SUMMARY

This teaching is about *letting go* of what is *outside* of you and trusting what is *inside*.

You are beginning to *release* the patterns of *isolation and separation* within you.

You are moving into your *heart*, accepting and valuing *who* you are as you move on to the pathway of the *unknown*.

As you continue to do the mirror exercise, you will begin to *enjoy* who you see reflected there, as opposed to *judging* and *shaming* yourself.

You will look in the mirror one day and say:

"I like this person. There must be something to this process!"

LESSON NINE

Take Charge of Your Life

INTRODUCTION

Life mastery is about realizing your *full potential* as a human being.

It involves the *full realization* of the self where you are able to see and know yourself in all your *uniqueness* and to grow to a place of full compassion, acceptance, expression, and love.

You are, in effect, *falling in love* with you.

If you can fall in love with yourself by acknowledging all the *unique* aspects of you, you can *take charge* of your life and take your *place* in the world.

Always remember this truth: *The love you have for yourself powers your ability to be you.*

I. TAKING YOUR PLACE IN THE WORLD (WORLD SERVICE)

You have questions about *world service.* You are not sure what world service is, what it involves or what it is supposed to be. You may be wondering, what *is* world service?

Or you may be thinking: "I have a hard enough time taking care of myself. How do I give myself to the world?"

The main thrust of this program is for you to *see* and *know* yourself. When you are able to *see* you and *be* you, you will be able to *choose* and *decide* how you will give your talents and gifts to the world—where it is not about

55

"me" any more. It is about *giving* what you know in the depth of your *heart* to the world in whatever fashion you choose.

That is why we give you the exercises and information in this program and ask you to fully *engage* with them—to bring you to a place of fully acknowledging the depth and breadth of *you,* so that you may move from your *mind* to your *heart.*

Your heart will guide you to your place in the world.

To learn to use your heart, you must move from your *old* way of being to the *new.*

II. FITTING IN VERSUS MAKING YOUR MARK

Committing to world service requires taking *all* of yourself into the world—what you decide you *do* love and what you *don't.*

You are looking out into the world asking, Where do I fit in?—as opposed to deciding to *make a mark* in the world by fully acknowledging you and your *unique* personal qualities, gifts, and talents.

How can you make your *unique* mark in the world if you are unable to acknowledge *all* the qualities that make you unique?

That is why it is important to continue to do these exercises. We ask you to continue the mirror exercise because it is time to look in the mirror and admit that it is a *challenge* for you to fully acknowledge *and* receive you.

When you look into the mirror and judge some things as lovable but others as *unacceptable,* you are telling the world you are *unlovable.* You are setting up a system of *duality* within yourself, saying:

"I can only show the world what I feel is loveable about me. I cannot show the world the part of me I consider *unlovable.*"

Your *conditioning* by those outside of you has determined where you see yourself as *unlovable.* Look outside of you and notice how you have set up a similar system of duality with *others* in your life where you only accept *parts* of them and cannot accept other parts. Look at where there is duality in you, and ask:

Can I find love for those aspects of me that I have decided are *unlovable?*

When you try to hide aspects of yourself from the world that you deem unlovable, you are simply trying to comfortably fit in.

EXERCISE ONE 🖎

1. Ask:

   • Where am I still trying to find a place in the world where I can comfortably *fit in,* as opposed to trying to *revolutionize* the world?

We use the word *revolutionize* because we are asking you to *broaden* your horizons, to think *bigger* than you ever have before.

We are asking you to open to the *possibilities* of the world outside of you by asking:

"Where can I expand the pathway of possibility for me?"

2. Write down this statement:

I am now revolutionizing my process and expanding the pathway of possibility for me!

Affirm this. What feelings come up for you?

3. You are choosing to move into your *greatness* and into the realm of *possibility.*

   • Why is it *important* to do this?

   • How *can* you do this?

   • What needs to be *changed* in your life to begin to *manifest* your uniqueness?

Through your *uniqueness* you can make a contribution with your *individual* stamp. It is not about *fitting in.*

So ask:

Can I *expand* and *revolutionize* my path as I move toward the realm of *possibility?*

Can I show up fully realized, self-sustained, individuated, and fully immersed in the realization of my unique self so that I may declare:

I AM that I AM, and here I AM!

III. LOVE YOURSELF

EXERCISE TWO ✍

1. You are beginning to define or redefine what love is for you and where your place in the world is based on love.

    You have done the mirror exercise to see *who* you really are and to see the aspects of yourself that have *blocked* you from truly seeing yourself. Look directly into your eyes and ask yourself:

    • *What* is love to me?

    • Am I fully *loving* me?

    • Am I fully *giving* to me?

    • Am I fully *dedicating* my life to me?

    • Or am I seeking to attain a certain *status* or *position* so I can be loved?

    • Where am I still *giving myself away* in order to be loved?

2. Write down *where* you are right now. Are you able to accept with *compassion* where you are?

   Your ability to accept with compassion where you are is an indication of how much you fully *love yourself.*

3. Now write down what you are *giving* to yourself.

   Ask:

   - What am I *giving* to myself that has true *meaning* and *value* for me?

   - You may ask, what does that *mean?*

   Your answers will reveal the true depth of *love* that you have for *yourself.* Be honest with yourself.

4. Set an intention where you state, "I am giving (be specific)_____to myself."

5. It is time for you to *receive* you. Look in the mirror and tell yourself how much you *love yourself,* and admire the *commitment* you have made to this program and to your growth.

SUMMARY

You are now in a place of *accepting* you and letting go of *indulging* yourself—indulging your *feelings* or languishing in the drama and glamour of *confusion.*

It is time to feel your feelings and to be decisive and clear.

It is time to *grow up.*

It is time to move from the womb of mom and the arms of dad to a place of full self-acceptance and individuation while being *decisive* about what you are moving toward.

It is time to *decide* where you are headed.

- Do you choose to allow your *vacillating feelings* to guide your life?

  Or

- Do you choose to *move toward* what you say you *want—toward blazing your own trail as a unique, individuated, wonderful creation?*

It is time to take charge of your life.

It is time to take hold of the *wounded* child and the *wonder* child and take them on this pathway, knowing they are *always with you.*

This is why we ask you to do the mirror exercise—to look at the parts of you that you *love* and those aspects of you that you have labeled *unlovable*—so that you may bring *both* these children with you.

Let go of struggling to *survive.*

Look at the road of *possibility* and make a decision to say:

"I am ready to be seen, to be loved, and to blaze this trail. I am taking charge of my life!"

Move Out into the World

INTRODUCTION

Through these teachings you are moving from *adolescence* into *adulthood.* That is why we have asked you to begin making decisions that support your *highest good.*

You are looking into the mirror and asking, What is important to me? With newfound aspects of yourself, you're making decisions based on what you say you *want.*

You are a self-contained entity, an energetic whole, capable of seeing *all* aspects of yourself, which you accept with *compassion.* You are beginning to look out at the masses with the *same* acceptance and compassion.

You are looking to move out into the world on a *new* pathway honoring and valuing you.

World service occurs when you begin to look for ways to *express* yourself and ask, What can I *give* to the world?

This lesson is about moving out into the world and into the *soul group* of your choice while maintaining the integrity of *yourself* as a self-contained entity.

I. DEVELOPING INDIVIDUAL AND GROUP RELATIONSHIPS

Old judgments and shame fall away as you *integrate* parts of yourself that you once *avoided* or *rejected*—by honoring and valuing you.

You are ready to *move out* into the world in *unity* with those outside of yourself with whom you are having a relationship—joining with others in world service, ensuring that you and what you have to say are *respected* as having equal value.

It is time to develop relationships and find groups with those who *resonate* with you and you with them. In a resonant community, you may share your vision, talents, and gifts and express yourself to the *fullest*. It is time to *be* you and to live in a *balance* of giving and receiving with like-minded individuals.

EXERCISE ONE 📬

A relationship is the *energetic entity* that is created and built by those individuals in the relationship. The health of a relationship is the responsibility of *all* the parties in it. Let us first look at the relationship you are having with *yourself*. Write your answers in your journal:

- Do I fully love, honor, and value *me?*

- Do I consciously seek to be *aware of* and *support* my highest good?

- Is there true *intimacy* in my relationship with my *self?*

- Does my relationship with *me* include sensitivity to *others?*

- What about my relationship with *myself* allows me to remain in *old* relationships that do *not* support my highest good?

Be with your answers and meditate on how your relationship with *yourself* reflects your relationships with *others*.

EXERCISE TWO ✍️

Now look at your *personal* relationships and ask:

- What *is* this relationship?

- Why am I *in* this relationship?

- Why is this relationship *important* to me?

- Why are some of my so-called relationships *unfulfilling*?

- Do I *resonate* with them and they with me?

- Is there a *balance* of giving and receiving?

- Am I in this relationship simply to remain in a *comfort zone*?

- Are we serving each other's *highest good*?

Use these questions to evaluate your current and future *personal* relationships. Add any questions you deem useful.

EXERCISE THREE ✍️

Now look at the *groups* you are involved with.

Ask any of the above questions that seem appropriate and add these:

- Do we have a sense of *group unity,* or is it more about *each person's* struggle for power?

- Can this group move toward a *common goal* and the greater good of the *whole*?

- Do the members *resonate* with me and I with them?

- Are we serving each other's *highest good* and honoring and valuing each other with a *balance* of giving and receiving?

- Are the opinions and ideas of group members *welcomed* and received *openly* and *equally?*

- Do I acknowledge and accept the opinions and ideas of *others?*

With both personal and group relationships, it is also useful to ask:

- Are these relationships being created and sustained with *love* and *nurturing?*

- Is it worth the *time* and *effort* to maintain and nurture these relationships?

Many of your so-called relationships may *fall away.* That is just another step in you taking *responsibility* for you.

II. CREATING HEALTHY RELATIONSHIPS

When there is a *balance* of giving and receiving, relationships can be created and nurtured with love, integrity, honesty, and truth.

Those who are *committed* to a relationship will foster and honor it by honoring each other as *individuals.*

You have been doing the exercises, and you are more aware of the degree to which you are honoring and valuing *yourself* and expressing your *truth.*

You are accepting with compassion *where* you are.

You now have a *foundation* that you can *build* upon.

You are clearer as to *what* you want where the good of the *whole* is concerned.

You can now create, foster, and nurture relationships in the microcosm by simply looking across the room at someone and seeing the *mirror.*

III. OPENING COMMUNICATION

It is now time to open communication with those outside of yourself from the foundation of *self- knowledge* you have built in this program.

You are developing a profound connection with your *senses,* which are empowering you to decide what is *accurate* and *true* for you.

You are moving from the narcissistic *wounded child* to an *adult* who honors and values who they are and gives fully from that foundation—so that you may develop healthy, well-balanced relationships.

As you become more unified *within* yourself, you are better prepared to build relationships in *unity* with others for world service and the greater good of the whole.

You are moving from a place of *"me"* to a place of *"we."*

Fully moving from "me" to "we" defines the journey to spiritual maturity and life mastery.

SUMMARY

Open your front door and step out from the barriers you have built to remain *safe* in your own little world.

Look at what is happening in your world each day and become *aware*.

Strip the insulation from around you and take off your *armor*.

Ask yourself, What do I feel?

- Some will feel like *running back*, shutting the door, locking the locks, and not wanting to come out.

- Some will feel fear, anger, and sadness.

- Some will *rise to the occasion*, stand in their power, and say, This resonates for me, and this does not resonate. I will now see life beyond the tip of my nose and immerse myself in it.

Move out of the *cocoon* of your own life and see the *opportunities* before you. To do that, you must see your patterns and attachments and make a decision that moving forward is more important than resisting and indulging in being a *victim*.

You are marching on the road of *possibility* into the *unknown*, being you and trusting that where you are is exactly where you are supposed to be and that is *good enough*.

It is time to *grow up* as an adult. When you make this decision, you will move into a place of *greatness* that you never imagined.

Find Your Joy

INTRODUCTION

You realize that looking *outside* of yourself for stimulation, gratification, and validation *no longer* works. You are on a journey to connect with the light *inside* you. Though this journey is taking you into *unknown* territory, you are *safe*.

You have all the tools you need to open your *heart and mind* to receive your *answers* and to receive *life*. You are ready to discover *why* you are here.

As you continue to expand the limits of your *comfort zones,* your life will now be about *constantly* beginning over.

The path forward is guided by what you *resonate* with, what brings you *joy*. That is why it is essential that you follow your feelings to your truth in your *heart*.

As you open to the depth of your heart, you will access deep feelings that help you to discover your talents and gifts and joyful ways to employ them.

Let *joy* guide you forward on your path.

EXERCISE ONE ✍️

This lesson is about *joy*. Are you *enjoying* life? Are you enjoying who you are *being* and *where* you are in your life right now? Are you enjoying moving *forward* toward what you say you want?

Or do you still try to *survive* aspects of your life, even perhaps enjoying *fighting* lack and limitation because this fight is *familiar* to you? Is it possible you are *confusing* joy with safety and security?

1. Write your answers to these questions in your journal.

    *   *What is* joy for me?

    *   *Where* is there joy in my life?

    *   Can I look at my talents and gifts and *feel* joy?

    *   Do my current *circumstances* and *relationships* bring me joy?

    *   Are there circumstances and relationships in my life that represent *old* habits, patterns, and attachments that *no longer resonate* for me and do *not* bring me joy?

2. Let's explore further the question, *What* is joy for me?

    *   Write down what joy *is* and what it *means* for you. Describe in detail a few *situations* in which you felt a wonderful joyousness.

    *   How does joy *feel?* What is your first *reaction* when you begin to *feel* joy?

    *   What *voices* come up that try to *edit* or *censor* your joy?

Joy simply means feeling fulfilled within the depth of your heart. It is you feeling fulfilled by giving your gifts and talents to the world simply by you being you.

Joy can be *stimulated* by people and situations around you, but it is never *received* from the outside. Joy is fulfillment from *within*. Joy is not learned. It cannot be taught. It just is. You naturally *are* joy.

Having looked at your joy, how much do you love *yourself* now?

EXERCISE TWO ✍🏻

To discover your *true* path, you must begin to feel and pay attention to what *resonates* for you and what does *not*. So we are going to ask you to look at the world *outside* of you and consider:

What *resonates* for me, and what does *not*?

Make two lists:

1.   Write five *aspects* of the world (characteristics and circumstances) that you no longer resonate with and prefer *not* to experience.

2.   Then look at the world, and list five aspects that you *love* and *desire* to experience.

3.   Look at your lists.

   •   Where do you spend *most* of your energy in both your *personal* and *working* lives—with what *does* or does *not* resonate?

   •   Are you trying to *figure out* why certain things no longer resonate for you so you can *find* a way that they will?

   Or

   •   Are you able to simply notice what does *not* resonate, *release* those things, and *move on* to what does?

Free yourself by learning to *let go* of what does *not* resonate, and *discover* and *embrace* what *does* resonate for you.

EXERCISE THREE ✍

Move *within* to an inner space of silence and meditation. Write your answers to these questions in your journal:

1. What are my *five* most important talents and gifts? A good place to discover your talents and gifts is to examine your *accomplishments* you identified in previous lessons. What gifts and talents did you use that brought you *joy*?

2. Examine your five choices. Get in touch with your *feelings.* Move at your own pace. No need to rush through this process. When you feel ready, write your responses to these questions:

    *   What do I do *well*?

    *   What do I *like* doing?

    *   *What* in my life brings me the greatest *joy*?

    *   What do I love *doing* that brings me *joy*?

    *   What is my *passion*?

    *   What have I always *dreamt* of doing that I might *like* to do?

Your responses may include two or twenty things. Revisiting these questions over time may produce some very *different* answers. Ferreting out your truth is a *process,* not a one-time exercise. Pay attention to what brings you *joy* in your daily life.

3. Zero in on the *most important* item on your list by asking:

    *   What do I *love* doing that brings me the greatest *joy* and raises the level of *resonance* in me when I am doing it?

You will know it because it radiates from the depth of your *heart.* Write your answer and simply *be* with it for a moment.

4. Have you discovered your *passion,* what you love *doing* that brings you the greatest amount of *joy?* Once you identify it, ask:

    *   How does it make me *feel?*

    *   Is this something I could do right *now?* If not now, why not? When?

SUMMARY

Move inside and *summarize* where you are right *now*. Do this frequently as you move toward the end of this program. (Use questions at end of lesson one to guide you.)

You may discover that your feelings *fluctuate*. Move into a place of greater *acceptance* and *compassion* for *where* you are.

Many of you may be feeling fear and trepidation because you are moving out of your *comfort zones*.

If you are having *negative* thoughts like, "I can't do that," ask yourself:

    *   What holds me in a space of not having, not doing, not being?

    *   How does this reflect *old* conditioning and beliefs?

No matter what you believe is holding you in lack and limitation, you do *not* have to defer to it. Trust that you can live your truth.

What *passion* came up for you?

This passion is available for you to give from the depth of your heart.

LESSON TWELVE

———◆———

Decide What You Want

INTRODUCTION

The lessons and exercises in this program have helped you clarify *who* you are.

Now it is time for you to *be* who you are while facing the *unknown*. You have a set of tools that will guide and support your movement toward what you say you want. Before you move forward, you must *decide* what you want and *commit* to that.

It is important to recognize that on your life journey, you are always doing only *one* of two things:

- You are *having* what you say you want,

  Or

- You are *avoiding the feelings* that are surfacing inside you (fear, rejection, etc.)

In order to have what you say you want, you must be willing to *feel* these feelings. For as you move forward toward what you say you want, your feelings will get stronger until they reach a *crescendo*.

All the *shadow* feelings you ever wanted to *avoid* will come to the fore, into the *light*. They are there for you to *embrace* and *integrate*. Avoiding them will only *block* your progress.

You may be feeling some trepidation about taking steps to create a new life. Much of your *old* life revolved around the myth of *control* and *safety*. Your thoughts focused on trying to *control* things to keep you "safe."

There is no safety in *lack* and *limitation*.

You no longer need to settle for that because now you know *who* you are. Everything "out there" continues to be *unknown*, but because you know who you are, you are ready to create a *new* life based upon what you *resonate* with. You are ready to make a *commitment* to what you say you want. It is time for you to *be* who you are.

Any fear you experience is just a fear of *feeling* your feelings as you *move* toward what you say you want and as you *do* what you say you are here to do.

EXERCISE

1. Write your answers to the following questions:

    *   *What* do I want?

    *   What do I want to *do* in the world?

    *   Am I *having* and *doing* what I say I want right *now*?

    *   Am I truly *having*, *living*, and *being* what I say I want?

    *   If not, what feelings am I *avoiding* that are keeping me from taking the *actions* I need to take to achieve what I want?

    *   Is my heart *open* to receive all that I want? (If it was, you would already have what you say you want.)

2. Now let's explore your *commitments* and *intentions*. Ground yourself with three deep breaths as we have taught you. Bring yourself to *where* you are in this moment. Write your answers to the following questions:

- What do I *say* I want?

- What do I *actually* want?

- Considering this, what would I say I *truly* want?

- What have I *said* that I wanted *all along*?

- Are these things the *same*?

- Am I *having* what I truly want?

- If not, what feelings am I *avoiding*?

3. When you are done writing, close your eyes, move within, and *picture* and *sense* yourself having, living, and being what you truly want. When the picture is clear, continue by asking:

- What am I *feeling*?

- Am I truly *feeling* the feelings that are coming up in me?

- Am I feeling not *good* enough, not *worthy* enough, not *perfect* enough?

- Am I looking *outside* of myself for something to validate and gratify me?

- Do I know *who* I am?

- Am I ready to take the next *steps* toward having what I say I want?

SUMMARY

Remember, this process is *not* a race. It begins with you offering *yourself* acceptance and compassion for *where* you are and for what you are *feeling* in the moment.

It is not about *getting* something or somewhere so you can feel validated or gratified.

It is about bringing your unique gifts, talents and personal qualities out into the world in a way that brings you joy and fulfillment.

This is *your* life, a life to *live,* a life to *give,* a life to *be.* Your *process* is your life.

We will continue to ask you to *feel* your feelings as you live your life.

Always consider:

- *Where* am I?

- *What* am I feeling?

- What do I *want?*

Now, ask yourself one final question:

How much do I *love* myself now?

Set Your Boundaries

INTRODUCTION

You are creating a *new* you. Inevitably, that will affect your *relationships,* which raises the issue of your personal *boundaries.*

Boundaries are energetic, emotional, and physical limits that you place between you and other people.

Many of you don't fully understand what boundaries are, so you may not understand how they can be *used* or *misused* in relationships.

Are your boundaries:

- *Nonexistent,* so that you lose your sense of yourself, ignore your needs, and say *yes* when you want to say *no?*

- *Rigid and unresponsive* to conditions, causing you to *isolate* yourself so that you frequently find yourself in *conflict* with others?

  Or

- *Flexible and responsive* to conditions, thus helping to *build* relationships?

You are learning to speak your *truth* so that you can look at another and simply say, "These are my boundaries."

To set appropriate boundaries, you must first honor and value *yourself* and your *truth.*

Boundaries are lines drawn in the sand, not cement, because they can and will *change*.

The idea is to base them upon honoring and valuing *you* and *where* you are in your life.

I. HONORING AND VALUING YOU

EXERCISE ONE 🖎

Write your answers to these questions:

- What are ten *aspects* of me that I love and value?

- How do I *demonstrate* that I honor and value these aspects of me?

- Can I set *boundaries* based upon what I honor, value, and love about me?

- Am I *telling* those outside of myself *who* I am, or am I assuming they know?

- Am I speaking my *truth* based upon who I am and what I honor and value?

II. CHANGE AND RELATIONSHIPS

Look at where your relationships are *changing* based upon the ten aspects of you that you love. As *you* have changed, have your *relationships* changed as well? Having *raised* the level of your resonance and vibration, do you now need to set *new* boundaries?

Look at what *no longer* resonates for you and what *does*. The ten aspects of what you *love* about yourself are places where you *resonate*. You have created a *new* you. *Who* is this new being?

Do the ten aspects you love reflect this new being?

You are beginning to *stand* in your power and to *move* forward and *manifest* what you want. You will continue to move forward as you learn more about *who* you are and *love* yourself more.

There is an important difference between knowing yourself through your *ego* (the old way) and through *self-love* (the new way). Knowing yourself through the ego is about *separating* yourself from others.

If you say, "I know who I am, and I am better than you," this is a form of *superiority,* and it creates *separation.* It creates a need for validation and gratification from *outside* of you.

Loving yourself as you *are,* on the other hand, allows you to stand *unmasked*—with your energy contained. It allows you to walk on the path into the unknown, unmasked, without creating *isolation.*

Having *boundaries* allows you to create a *balance* of giving and receiving in relationships. It means you can say, "I love me and, therefore, I can love you. Thus, our relationship has balance and equality. It empowers me to speak my *truth* when I need to set a *limit* or take care of myself, and it empowers you to do the *same* with me."

Boundaries are part of the foundation of community, harmony and equality. They lead to clear agreements and to having your needs met.

EXERCISE TWO ✍

1. List and define your *boundaries* in your *personal* and *professional* lives, especially as they relate to the *ten aspects* you love and value about yourself that you identified in the last exercise.

2. Then ask:

   • Am I setting *boundaries,* or am I building *walls* to isolate and separate myself?

   • Am I honoring and respecting the boundaries of *others* as well as my *own?*

SUMMARY

Look at what you have *accomplished* and *created* for yourself. Notice how these accomplishments reflect aspects of your self that you *love* and *value*.

Look at your life as being *full*. Are you walking on your path into the unknown feeling *joyful* about what you are creating within yourself?

Look at your life and see what you love about yourself. In the mirror, look directly into your eyes and begin to *receive* who you are now. Love *yourself* so you can begin to take the next step to loving *others*.

By committing to *knowing* and *loving* yourself on a deeper level, you have committed to individuate and to take responsibility for yourself. Setting boundaries is another step in taking *responsibility* for you.

Let Your Gifts and Talents Reveal Your Joy

INTRODUCTION

You have reached the point in this program and your life where you must decide to make a *leap* into a *new* life or *remain* where you are.

You know who you are, and you are ready to put why you are here into action.

But before you can do that, you must commit even more fully to discover your *gifts* and *talents*.

Fortunately, as every gift and talent is *revealed* to you, a *coinciding* feeling of *joy* will also be revealed to you.

You are uncovering gifts and talents that *resonate* with you in the depths of your *heart*.

This is why we have asked you and are asking you again: *What do you enjoy?*

EXERCISE ONE 🖎

1. Write your answers in your journal:

    • What do I enjoy *doing?*

    • What gifts and talents am I *using* when doing these activities?

    • Have I recognized these gifts and talents *before?*

- Where *else* have I enjoyed using these gifts and talents?

- *Which* gifts and talents best express *who* I am?

2. As you do what you do, notice if you are *enjoying* it. If you are, investigate where the *passion* is in this activity. Two questions are helpful:

    - Would I rather be doing something *else?*

    - If I wasn't doing this, what would I *prefer* doing?

3. It is time to focus on the meaning, value, and purpose of *everything* you do. So ask yourself when you are involved in an activity:

    - *Why* am I doing this?

    - What is the *meaning, value, and purpose* of this activity?

    - Is it to *get* something or to *give* something?

    - Is it to *prove* who I am, or am I *being* who I am?

    - Am I giving from the depths of my heart to *serve* the greater good?

    - Am I finding *joy* and *fulfillment* in this activity?

EXERCISE TWO ✍️

During the next week, make *two* lists side by side.

1. Each day write five *aspects* of you that you *love.*

2. Then make a list of your *gifts* and *talents.*

Creating both of these lists side by side will help you relate to and embody your talents and gifts in a brand *new* way. You will begin to see more clearly the *connection* between what you *love* about you and what you *enjoy doing* and do *well.*

When you make that connection, you allow your gifts and talents to reveal your joy.

SUMMARY

Look for ways to *embrace* and *embody* your gifts and talents and to *give* them to the world.

You are your gifts and talents.

By knowing and developing your gifts and talents, you will be able to *manifest* what you want simply by you *being* you.

Paint Your New Picture

INTRODUCTION

Your *tools*, *gifts*, and *talents* are the "brushes" you may use to paint the *new* picture of the life and world you say you want.

Your *heart* will tell you what *content* should be in your picture.

By paying attention to what and who *resonates* for you, you will be able to create your *new* life, form your new *soul family*, and develop the new world of *community*, *harmony*, and *equality* you desire.

EXERCISE ONE ✍

1. Since your gifts and talents are key, once again we ask you to make a list of *five* specific gifts and talents you are using to create your *new* life and world. Then answer these questions:

   • What am I doing for my *self* with my gifts and talents?

   • Which of these gifts and talents also help me serve the *world*?

   • When I am *giving* to the world, am I *receiving* love in return?

     Or

   • Am I using my talents and gifts to *get*—to keep me safe and secure, to survive, or to overcome lack and limitation?

   • Am I getting only enough in return for my giving to *survive* life?

- Is the way I am using my talents and gifts simply perpetuating *old* habits, patterns, and attachments?

2.   Reflect on your answers and then answer these questions:

- What am I *feeling* when I *recognize* my gifts and talents?

- What am I *feeling* when I *give* and when I *receive?*

- What am I *feeling* if I give only to *get?*

If you are giving only to *get,* you are still stuck in the *personal* self. When you have surrendered to *self-love,* the self expands in consciousness beyond the personal self and begins to desire to contribute to *others* through your gifts and talents—your greatest gift.

This exercise will help you begin to perceive the truth of what you are doing, so as you move forward in your *new* life, it will include a *balance* of giving and receiving.

To create that *balance,* you must recognize your talents, your gifts, and your value.

II. LOVE YOURSELF

EXERCISE TWO ✍️

Lets look again at how much you really *love* and *value* yourself.

- Do you love *who* you are now?

- Do you love *what* you have discovered about yourself?

- Do you love *whom* you have discovered?

- Do you love the wonderful *soul* who is expressing your talents and gifts?

Your answers will tell you *where* you are now.

III. DISCOVER YOURSELF

You have just begun to *scratch the surface* of a continuous process of *self-discovery*. This process is *never* finished.

Who you are manifests every *moment* of every day.

As you increase awareness of your gifts and talents by going into your *heart*, they will *solidify* and *grow*. You will continuously *rediscover* who you are in the process.

EXERCISE THREE 🖎

Before you go to bed each night, *review* and *meditate* (without judgment) about your day. Reflect on these questions:

- *Where* am I?

- What *transpired* today?

- Can I *accept* what transpired today?

- What have I *learned* about others and myself?

- What did I learn about my *talents* and *gifts* and how I *use* them?

- Which talents and gifts did I *use* to create the *new* life I desire?

- Can I move *within* and deepen my *love* of who I am, so I can now begin to *create* my *new* soul family?

Begin to notice how you are *responding* to whatever happens.

- Are you continuing your *old* habits, patterns, and rituals?

  Or

- Are you getting in touch with what you *resonate* with?

It is important to do this exercise daily to entrain your energy and teach you to *focus* on what you are *creating*.

This meditation will help you fully encompass all that you are with acceptance and compassion for *where* you are.

III. YOU ARE YOUR GIFTS AND TALENTS

You may have the misconception that your talents and gifts are specific *skills* you can use to *do* something for others or that enable you to *get* something.

But you can see now how you are using your talents and gifts in every *moment,* in every *situation,* and in every *interaction* with others.

Your gifts and talents are not only *skills* you employ. They are also you simply *being* who you are.

They are what you use to express your *being*—tools that you use to express the *essence* of you.

Giving of *who* you are through your talents and gifts allows *others* to find out who they are so they can *be* who they are.

Then they can find *their* talents and gifts and relay them to *others* just as you are doing.

SUMMARY

When we ask you to review your day, *release* shame and judgment and *stop* scrutinizing your every move.

You are where you are and are *exactly* where you are supposed to be in your process.

Ask:

- Can I *accept* this with compassion?

- Can I joyfully accept *where* I am?

- Can I commit to continually *changing* where I am?

The ability to change where you are is the key to creating your new life and world.

Create Your New Life with Joy

INTRODUCTION

This program was designed to help you see that *you* are the *creator,* the *source,* and the *power* of you.

You need nothing *outside* yourself in the physical to determine *who* you are or to *validate* or *gratify* you.

It is the love and truth *within* that is most important.

It is this love and truth that powers your *courage* to be you.

Meditate daily on this truth, and *be* who you are.

You Are Ready

You are ready to *choose* where your life is headed and to *release* having to look outside of yourself to see what everyone *out there* is doing.

You are releasing being a *follower* so that you can move into the depth of your power, greatness, and self knowing, so you may lead yourself by tapping into your *inner truth*—what *resonates* for you.

Having made the decision to walk within the energy of the *new,* you now have a chance to *release* every last remnant of the *old.* But as the new energy *mixes* with the old, you are likely to feel *anxious* and *unsettled* for a time. The door behind you is sealed shut, but the door to the future is still *unlocking.*

Your future will now be created by you.

You're still discovering *why* you are here, asking, "How will I use my gifts and talents?" Your answers will begin to *reveal themselves* as you concentrate on moving *forward* on your path toward your new life.

You are beginning to connect with your soul's *divine plan* in your *heart.* Be assured that the pathway you are on leads to it. Some people are further along than others, but *everyone reading this* is on their unique path.

Your soul plan unfolds as you embody your gifts and talents.

Look at yourself in the mirror. You can see there is *no turning back.* This is why your feelings are becoming more *intense.* You *resist* moving toward the life you say you want because you have moved out of your *comfort zones* where you were looking *outside* of yourself for validation and gratification. Nothing *outside* of you can gratify you any longer. This may *frighten* you. Where do you go for your answers?

Look inside *yourself.* Use what you have *within* you as your well of fulfillment. What you created by doing the exercises in this program is *in* your well. The well inside you is filled with *who* you are. The well will continue to fill as you discover more of your talents and gifts. Draw on this *reserve* as you create your *new* world of community, harmony, and equality.

You are resonating and vibrating at a new level. You may still be trying to hold on to *old* relationships that no longer *resonate* with the *new* you. Can you open up to the *unknown* and let the wonderful souls *come to you* who are your *new* soul family? Are you willing to release *old* relationships that do *not* fulfill your needs and create *new* relationships with those who resonate with the *new* you?

EXERCISE ✍❚

1. Continue writing down five aspects of your talents and gifts that you *love.*

2. Continue your nightly *meditation* where you reminisce about events of your day.

    - *What* did you learn about yourself and others?

    - *Where* did you use or not use your gifts and talents?

- Are you continuing *old* habits and patterns, or are you consciously choosing what *resonates* for you?

- Are you *giving* to yourself? Giving to yourself includes making *choices* that serve your highest good. Do something *good* for yourself every day.

You are on a *new* pathway. For some, the pathway appears *empty*. For others, it is filling up with new *opportunities* and *people* who *resonate* with you and are open to you if you stay open.

Release in your life what *no longer serves* you. Stay alert to where you are expending energy in ways that do *not* move you toward the life you want.

As you love yourself more, you will do the things necessary to take care of yourself *mentally, emotionally, physically,* and *spiritually*. That is what loving yourself *means*.

Reach out to like-minded individuals for support and guidance as you move forward in your process. The old pattern was, "I can do this alone." This is no longer a viable option. Always remember the need for *community*.

As you create your new soul family, be aware of your old biological family patterns where separation, isolation, and duality existed. The new soul family embraces *community, harmony, equality, acceptance, and love from your heart*.

Allow yourself the freedom of full self-expression:

- State your *needs*.

- Speak your *truth* with no intention to harm.

- Set your *boundaries*.

- *Be* who you are.

You are ready to live your life for *you*.

Now create your new life with *joy*.

You are ready!

Law of Attraction

Although the teachings in *Life Mastery* have a spiritual source, we generally have taken a secular approach in presenting them because they have a practical application in our lives that doesn't require a spiritual context for us to understand and apply them. We, of course, reveal from the beginning that the source for these teachings is the Archangelic Realm of Michael.

One important spiritual teaching in the original source material, not included in this program, is popularly called the *Law of Attraction*. This law refers to the effect of *consciousness* on energy and manifestation. *Life Mastery* is about creating *new* levels of consciousness as we undertake the mission of creating the life we want and the courage to live it. So understanding the role consciousness plays in *attracting* the energies we wish to manifest in our life is not only relevant, it is essential.

Archangel Michael tells us, "When you love, honor, and value yourself and know who you are, you begin to vibrate at a higher level, drawing people and circumstances to you consistent with the new level of vibration."

That is the *Law of Attraction*, and here, briefly, is how it works:

Everything on Earth has an energetic frequency that connects to the frequency that *matches* it. Energy flows in the direction of and *connects* with the energy that attracts it. Our consciousness creates a field of attraction that *magnetizes* energy to us, allowing corresponding energetic frequencies to *attach* themselves to us.

The energy of fear attracts fear. The energy of love attracts love. All energies contained within these two polarities attract *similar* frequencies. When we focus on our unworthiness, imperfections, and fears, we unconsciously *project* that into the world and *attract* these lower frequencies to us.

On the other hand, the awareness of ourselves as *divine* expressions of power and worthiness attracts *higher* frequencies that manifest as joy, peace, and abundance. In essence, we create what we *focus* on. So we must choose carefully and be aware of what we focus on.

Choosing our awareness (consciousness) sets an *intention* for our energetic frequency. There are many energies to choose from, and *all* are possible connections and expressions for us. So pay attention to the consciousness you *choose* for yourself. Energy has no judgment or opinion. It is simply attracted and attaches to a *corresponding* frequency.

Be aware of yourself as *divine,* and you will connect with the *highest* energetic frequencies that allow your divinity to *manifest.* Consciously reject fear, and it will *not* exist as an option for you. Let your consciousness choose joy, peace, abundance, and love, and that is the reality you will *attract* and create for yourself.

That is what *Life Mastery* teaches us to do.

Links

The Second Coming: The Archangel Gabriel Proclaims a New Age, with Channel Robert Baker

http://www.gabrielsecondcoming.com

http://www.facebook.com/GabrielTheSecondComing

Life Mastery: A Guide for Creating the Life You Want and the Courage to Live It, with Channel Jeff Fasano

http://www.facebook.com/TheLifeMasteryProgram

The Ascension Handbook: A Guide to Your Ecstatic Union with God, with Channel Jessie Keener

http://www.facebook.com/TheAscensionHandbook

The Angel News Network

http://www.theangelnewsnetwork.com

http://www.facebook.com/TheAngelNewsNetwork

www.ingramcontent.com/pod-product-compliance
Lightning Source LLC
Chambersburg PA
CBHW081153090426
42736CB00017B/3297